This book is dedicated to you, who is extra specially different.

Most stories start with "Once upon a time..."
But not this one.
This story starts with a big HELLO!

Hello,
I'm Lamb!

Nice to meet you, friend!

When you see a lamb,
you might think we're all the same.

But I am different,
and have been all along.

Being different used to worry me.

But a certain shepherd changed the way I feel...

Shall I tell you how?

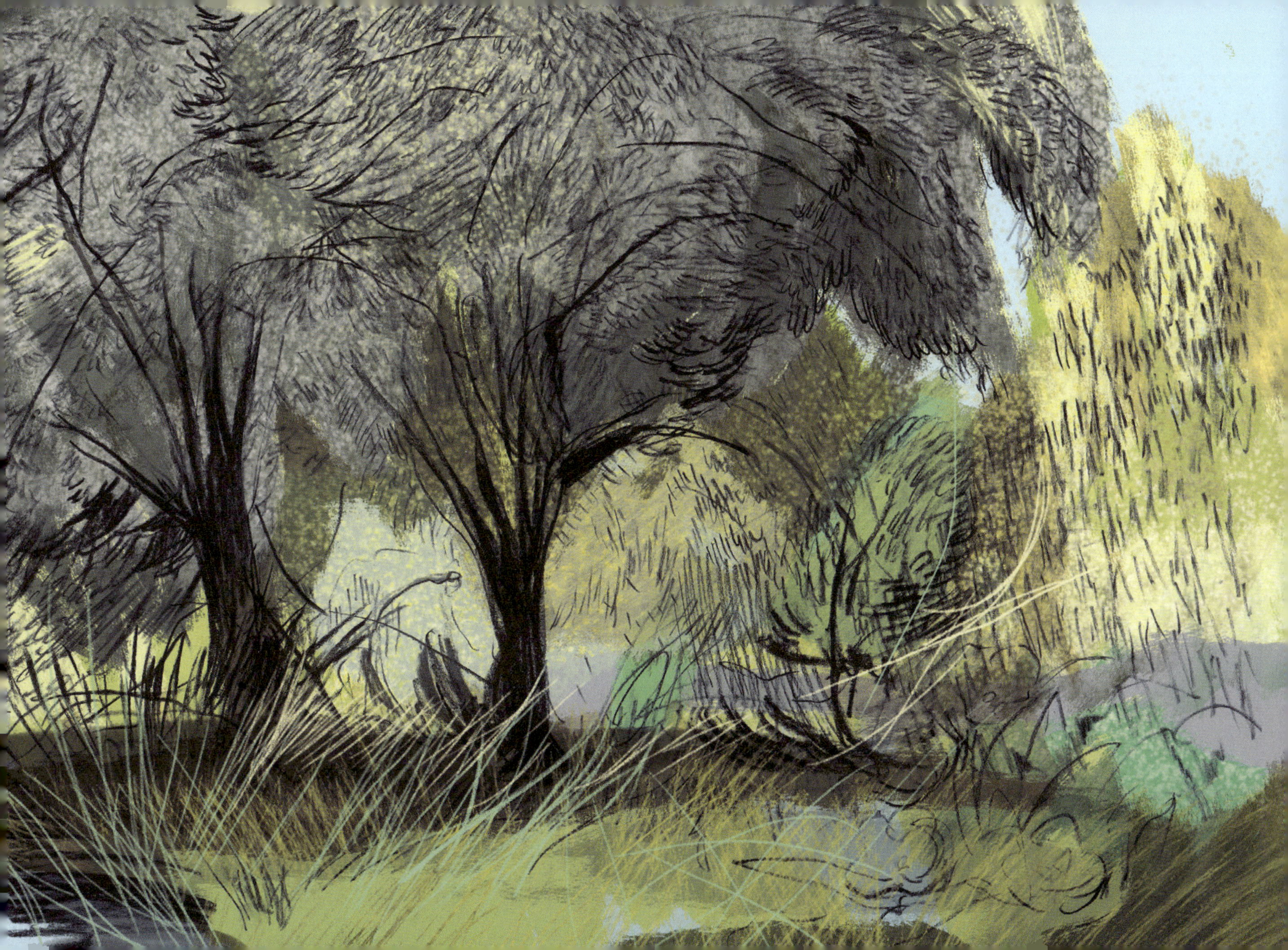

I was always a curious lamb,
wondering about things:

"What would happen if..."
or
"What's behind that fence?"

My mind would wander and I'd get lost in my thoughts -

so many that I couldn't even count them.

I'd explore in my own exciting world,

and try exciting new adventures.

I hid from Mummy Sheep then called out for her to find me.

That was fun!

(Although Mummy didn't think so!)

I jumped in the air as high as I could just to see if I would land again. Somehow I did every time!

I lay down on the soft grass and looked up at the sky.

Have you ever done that? Lifted your eyes up high?

Fluffy lambs ran across the blue. They changed their shape so quickly and ran so fast they flew!

Once, I climbed a great big hill where I could see for miles.

So many things to look for -
so much to explore!

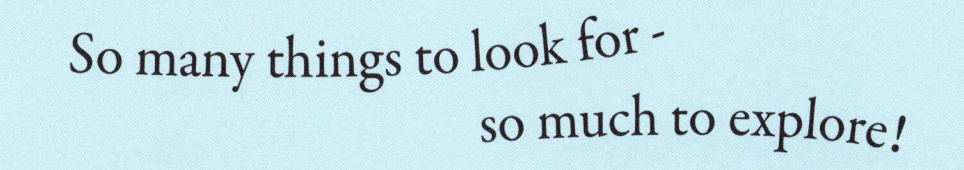

Different shapes and colours,

new sounds and exciting smells to find.

While the other lambs were eating grass
and didn't want to follow me,
I went exploring in a big muddy hollow.

To take a closer look
I had to climb in further,

but soon my feet were stuck
and the more I wriggled,
the deeper in the muck I sank.

That's when the shepherd
came and took me by the tail...

"Back to Mummy Sheep!"

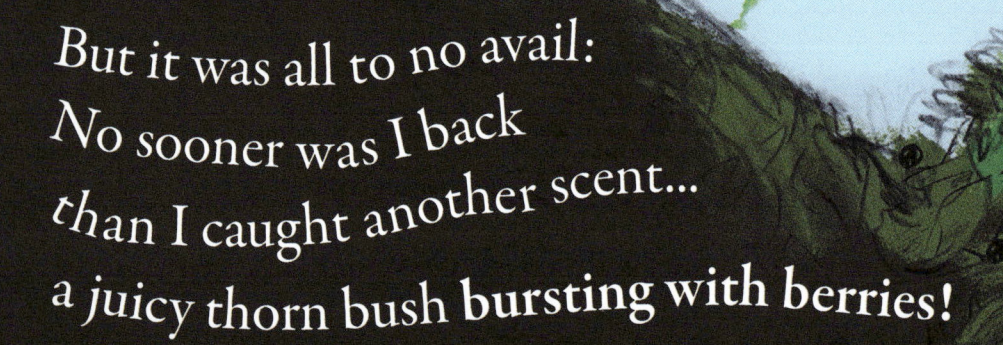

But it was all to no avail:
No sooner was I back
than I caught another scent...
a juicy thorn bush **bursting with berries!**

To get the best ones
I had to climb right in...

Stuck again!
Off to look for me the shepherd went!

I called out for him.
Then just before the sunset
I heard the shepherd's voice
and felt his hand gently free me.

Sometimes other lambs were mean and whispered beastly things.

But I could hear them all chewing grass and grumbling.

Mummy Sheep said to me
they didn't see the world like me.
she said that I was special,
she said I was unique.

But I didn't like the whispering,
I didn't want to be unique.

Being different worried me.

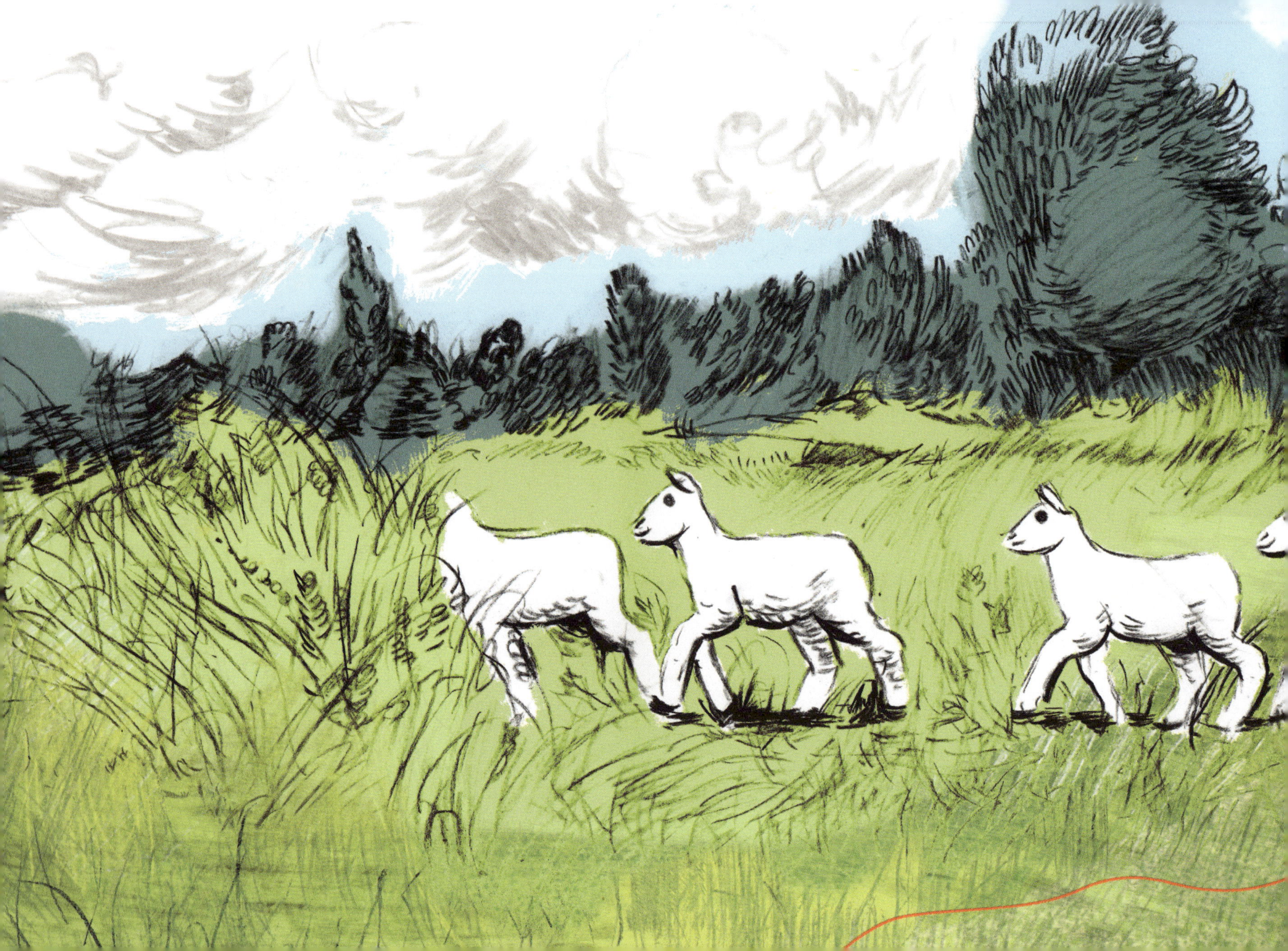

So I tried to be like other lambs,
I tried and tried and tried!
But every time I tried again,
something else would catch my eye.

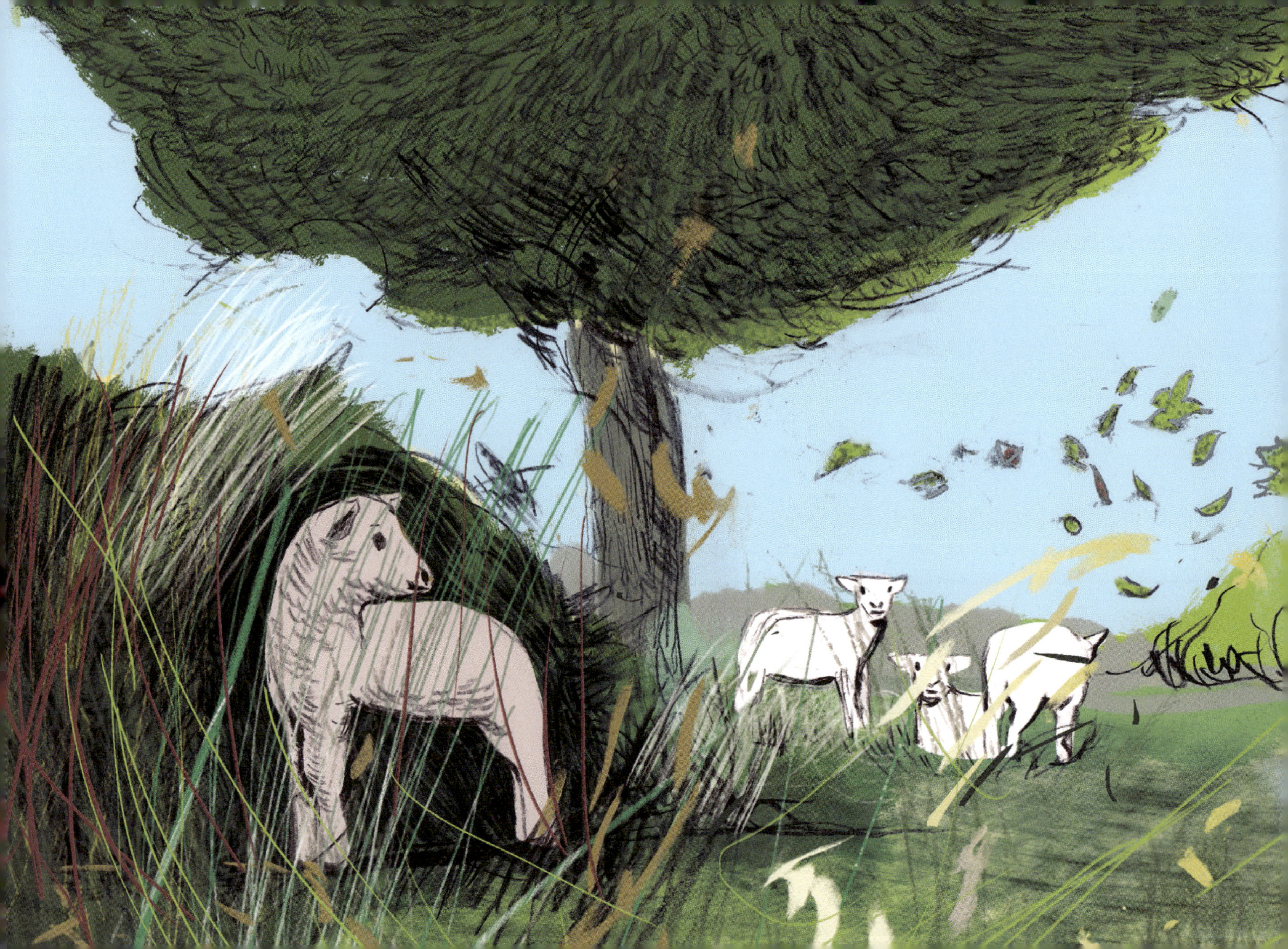

Leaves floated on the breeze and sang sweet songs to me, stars would run and hide and make me chase them endlessly. No matter how hard I tried I couldn't seem to stop; It really made me struggle trying to fit into the flock.

Mummy Sheep could sense
that fitting in had made me sad
so she asked if I would follow her
to where the shepherd sat.

He was sitting talking,
sharing stories by the fire
of muddy hollows, prickly bushes,
singing leaves and playful stars.

Each and every story he shared about me
he told with love and laughter,
so happy and carefree!

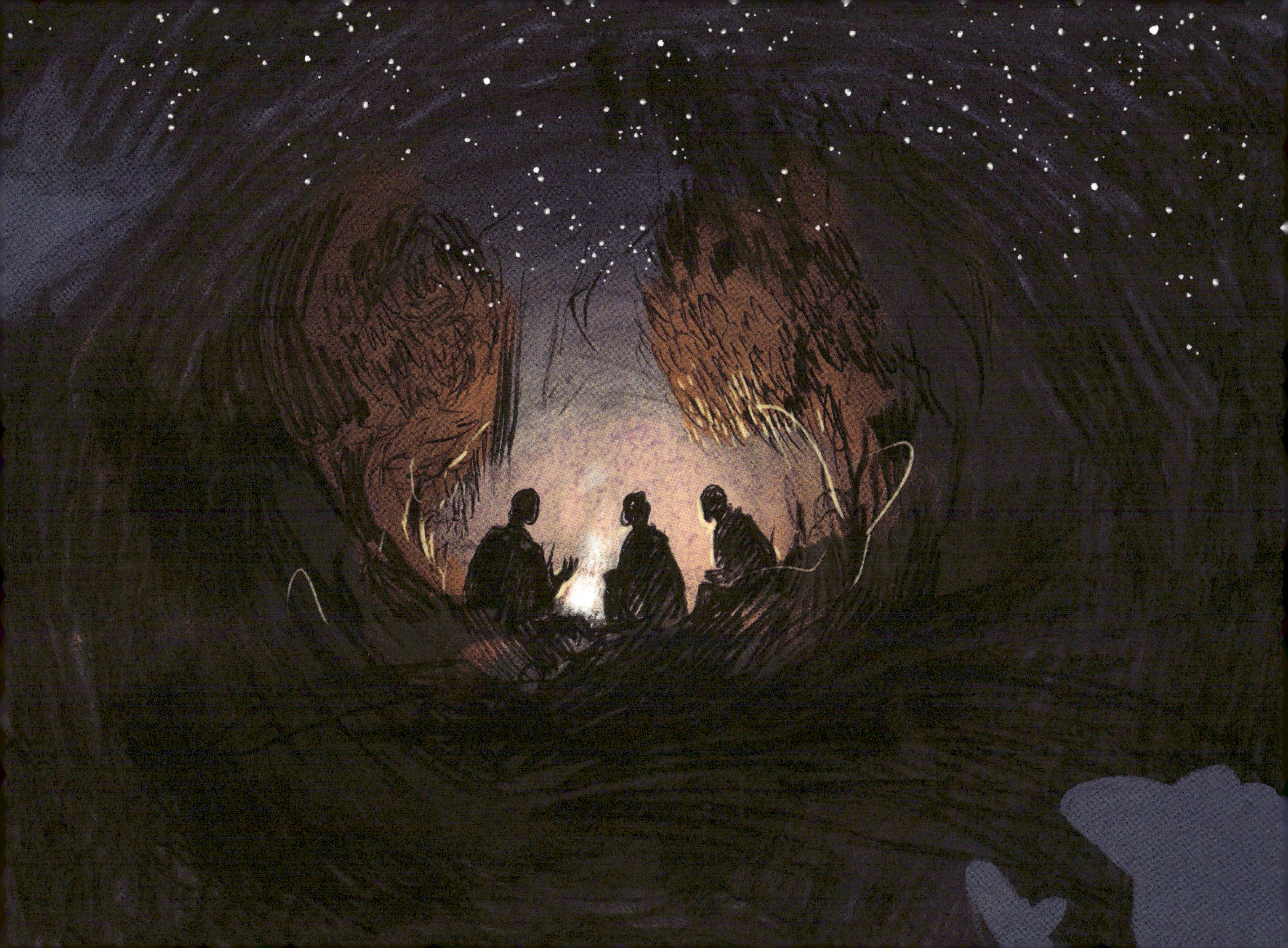

Then the shepherd turned
and fed me from his hand.

He smiled, and kindly said to me,

"Sweet lamb, you are different
and I know that makes you sad,
but listen to my voice.
I love you just the way you are."

That felt so good to me
it made me feel all fuzzy.

Being different used to worry me,
but this had set me...

free!

Happily different

and ready to dream.

CRS